P9-DLZ-304

ks.com

ks trademark is owned by Castle Point Publications, LLC.
published and distributed by St. Martin's Press.

(paper over board)
(ebook)

s Campbell

ma Parish

ased in bulk for promotional, educational,
ntact your local bookseller or the
Premium Sales Department at 1-800-221-7945,
ail at MacmillanSpecialMarkets@macmillan.com.

YOU CA

TF

CONTENTS

SPEAKING THE RUTH
TO AMERICA

THERE'S JUST SOMETHING ABOUT THE NOTORIOUS RBG,
a.k.a. Ruth Bader Ginsburg. She's tough as nails in her dissents
and in the gym [at 85 years old!]. She rocks the Supreme Court
and social media memes. While attending law school, she
cared for a newborn and saw her husband through intensive
cancer treatments. She's beaten cancer twice and wears a
jabot like none other.

As a US Supreme Court Justice [the second woman to be
appointed], Ginsburg has been outspoken and instrumental
in advancing reproductive rights, gender equality, healthcare
access, and same-sex marriage. But RBG began crashing ceilings
and barriers well before her Supreme Court confirmation.

At a time when only a handful of women went to law school,
RBG graduated first in her class at Columbia in 1959. Yet she
still faced gender discrimination from firm after firm when
seeking employment. Instead of letting the experience bring
her down, she used it to steel herself and seek places where

she could make a difference throughout her distinguished career. One of those trailblazing moments: Ginsburg cofounded the Women's Rights Project at the ACLU, for which she argued landmark cases on gender equality before the US Supreme Court. Her appointment to the US Court of Appeals in 1980 was a springboard to her appointment to the Supreme Court in 1993—and her infamous dissents.

Ginsburg proves that disagreeing does not make one disagreeable. She's respected and beloved by many—including her ideological opposition. RBG was easily confirmed by the Senate [96-3], and former Supreme Court Justice Antonin Scalia was her dear friend. Ginsburg's wisdom has never been more relevant or more important to American democracy. Let RBG's words on law and life give you courage to stand up and say, "I dissent."

My objective was to take the Court
step by step to the realization,
in Justice Brennan's words,

THAT THE PEDESTAL ON WHICH SOME THOUGHT WOMEN WERE STANDING ALL TOO OFTEN TURNED OUT TO BE A CAGE.

Interview with the *New Republic*,
September 2014

It takes people, **MEN AS WELL AS WOMEN**, who appreciate that there is a family life as well as a home life to be lived, and press for change.

Symposium at Columbia Law School,
February 10, 2012

As a litigator . . . I would try to get men on the bench to think not so much about what good husbands and fathers they were, but about how they wanted the world to be **FOR THEIR DAUGHTERS AND GRANDDAUGHTERS.**

Gruber Distinguished Lecture in Women's Rights,
hosted by Yale Law School,
October 19, 2012

Women will have achieved true equality when men share with them the responsibility of bringing up the next generation.

Interview with ABC News correspondent Lynn Sherr, November 15, 2000

PERHAPS THE LARGEST CHALLENGE IS **TO MAKE IT POSSIBLE FOR PEOPLE TO THRIVE IN BOTH A WORK LIFE AND A FAMILY LIFE.** THERE'S VERY LITTLE A COURT CAN DO TO SOLVE THAT PROBLEM. LEGISLATION LIKE THE FAMILY AND MEDICAL LEAVE ACT CAN ADVANCE CHANCES FOR PEOPLE TO HAVE A SATISFYING WORK LIFE AND, AT THE SAME TIME, A FULFILLING FAMILY LIFE.

Gruber Distinguished Lecture in Women's Rights, hosted by Yale Law School, October 19, 2012

I passed a door this morning
that said "Lactation Room."
How the world has changed.

Symposium at Columbia Law School,
February 10, 2012

I remain an advocate of the **Equal Rights Amendment** for this reason. I have a daughter and a granddaughter.

US Supreme Court Justice
Confirmation Hearings,
July 20-23, 1993

WOMEN'S RIGHTS ARE AN ESSENTIAL PART OF THE OVERALL HUMAN RIGHTS AGENDA, trained on the equal dignity and ability to live in freedom all people should enjoy.

Via the American Civil Liberties Union [ACLU]

Every modern human rights
document has a statement
that men and women
are equal before the law.
Our Constitution doesn't.

US Supreme Court Justice
Confirmation Hearings,
July 20-23, 1993

THE ANNOUNCEMENT THE PRESIDENT JUST MADE IS SIGNIFICANT, I BELIEVE, because it contributes to the end of the days when women, at least half the talent pool in our society, appear in high places only as one-at-a-time performers.

US Supreme Court Justice
Nomination Acceptance Address,
June 14, 1993

It is certainly a fundamental human right that men and women should have the chance to pursue whatever is their God-given talent, **and not be held back simply because they're male or female.**

Interview with ABC News correspondent Lynn Sherr, November 15, 2000

I do believe that Thomas Jefferson, were he alive today, would say that **WOMEN ARE EQUAL CITIZENS.**

US Supreme Court Justice
Confirmation Hearings,
July 20–23, 1993

Growing up, I never saw a woman in a symphony orchestra. Someone came up with the bright idea—let's drop a curtain between the people who are auditioning and the judges. . . . Almost overnight, women were making their way into symphony orchestras. Now, I wish we could duplicate the dropped curtain in every area. . . . How you get past that kind of unconscious bias . . . even today remains a difficulty.

Stanford Rathbun Lecture,
February 6, 2017

Restrictions we now see as discriminatory,
keeping women in a confined space,
were regarded as designed to protect
and care for the weaker sex. So, we had
to be clear in showing, concretely, how
these classifications harm everyone:
men, women, and children.

Gruber Distinguished Lecture in Women's Rights,
hosted by Yale Law School,
October 19, 2012

I count as the most significant legal activities I have pursued my work in comparative law and toward **THE ADVANCEMENT OF EQUAL OPPORTUNITY AND RESPONSIBILITY FOR WOMEN** and men in all fields of human endeavor.

Senate Judiciary Committee Initial Questionnaire
[Supreme Court], 1993

I think **daughters** can change the perception of their **fathers.**

Yahoo! interview with Katie Couric,
July 30, 2014

What is the difference between a New York City garment district bookkeeper and a Supreme Court Justice? One generation my life bears witness, the difference between opportunities open to my mother, a bookkeeper, and those open to me.

> Remarks presented to the
> Spertus Institute of Jewish Studies,
> September 13, 2009

The decision whether or not to bear a child is central to a woman's life, to her well-being and dignity. **It is a decision she must make for herself.**

US Supreme Court Justice
Confirmation Hearings,
July 20-23, 1993

Reproductive choice has to be straightened out. **THERE WILL NEVER BE A WOMAN OF MEANS WITHOUT CHOICE ANYMORE. . . . SO WE HAVE A POLICY THAT AFFECTS ONLY POOR WOMEN,** and it can never be otherwise, and I don't know why this hasn't been said more often.

Interview with the *New York Times*,
July 7, 2009

Many of today's young women think the day has come for genuinely protective laws and regulations. Were the legislature filled with women, I might have more faith in that proposition.

US Supreme Court Justice
Confirmation Hearings,
July 20-23, 1993

FREE TO BE

HOW CAN I DESCRIBE THE AMERICAN DREAM?

Maybe it's captured by the first ride I took on a
New York subway, after returning from several
months in Sweden, where everybody looked the
same, and here I was on the subway, and the
amazing diversity of the people of the United States.
You know the motto is *E pluribus unum* – "Of many,
one" – and that's the idea that, more than just
tolerating, we can appreciate our differences and
yet pull together for the long haul.

Interview with the
American Academy of Achievement,
July 14, 2016

LIKE SO MANY OTHERS,
I OWE SO MUCH TO
THE ENTRY THIS NATION
AFFORDED TO PEOPLE
**"YEARNING TO
BREATHE FREE."**

US Supreme Court Justice
Confirmation Hearings,
July 20–23, 1993

I TRY TO TEACH THROUGH MY OPINIONS,

through my speeches, how wrong it is to judge people on the basis of what they look like, color of their skin, whether they're men or women.

Interview with Irin Carmon on
The Rachel Maddow Show,
February 16, 2015

This is a very trying issue for our time: the individual's right to be free and the individual's respect for others. One hopes that we can reason together and get the message of **mutual respect** across to our young people.

> US Supreme Court Justice
> Confirmation Hearings,
> July 20-23, 1993

A PERSON'S BIRTH STATUS should not enter into the way that person is treated.

US Supreme Court Justice
Confirmation Hearings,
July 20–23, 1993

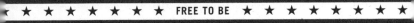

I SEE MY ADVOCACY AS PART OF AN EFFORT TO MAKE THE EQUALITY PRINCIPLE EVERYTHING the founders would have wanted it to be if they weren't held back by the society in which they lived and particularly the shame of slavery.

Interview with *The Takeaway*,
September 12, 2013

Since the start of the 1970s, it has been my consistent policy to refuse to attend professional or social functions at clubs that do not have nondiscriminatory admission policies.

Senate Judiciary Committee Initial Questionnaire
[Supreme Court], 1993

I APPRECIATE THAT THE UNITED STATES **IS A COUNTRY OF MANY RELIGIONS.**

US Supreme Court Justice
Confirmation Hearings,
July 20-23, 1993

THIS COUNTRY IS GREAT BECAUSE OF ITS ACCOMMODATION OF DIVERSITY.

US Supreme Court Justice
Confirmation Hearings,
July 20–23, 1993

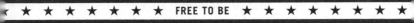

There can be a **HAPPY WORLD**
and there will be once again,
when men create a strong bond
towards one another, **A BOND
UNBREAKABLE** by a studied
prejudice or a passing circumstance.

Bulletin of the East Midwood Jewish Center,
June 21, 1946

I am alert to discrimination.
I grew up during World War II in
a Jewish family. I have memories
as a child, even before the war,
of being in a car with my parents
and passing . . . a resort with
a sign out in front that read:
"No dogs or Jews allowed."

US Supreme Court Justice
Confirmation Hearings,
July 20-23, 1993

We live in a democracy
that has, through the years,
**BEEN OPENED PROGRESSIVELY
TO MORE AND MORE PEOPLE.**

US Supreme Court Justice
Confirmation Hearings,
July 20-23, 1993

The most dangerous thing the government can do is to try to censor speech on the basis of the viewpoint that is being expressed.

US Supreme Court Justice
Confirmation Hearings,
July 20-23, 1993

The message of the first amendment is tolerance of speech, not the speech we agree with, but the speech we hate.

US Supreme Court Justice
Confirmation Hearings,
July 20-23, 1993

Freedom to **THINK, SPEAK,** and **WRITE** are so precious but also vulnerable.

World Justice Forum V,
July 10, 2017

We have constitutional
rights and one can't be
punished for exercising
a constitutional right.
**Otherwise, the right
is not real.**

US Supreme Court Justice
Confirmation Hearings,
July 20-23, 1993

The richness of the diversity of this country is a treasure, and it is a constant challenge, too, **a challenge to remain tolerant and respectful of one another.**

US Supreme Court Justice
Confirmation Hearings,
July 20-23, 1993

Yes, there are
miles in front,
**but what a distance
we have traveled.**

US Supreme Court Justice
Senate Confirmation Hearings,
July 20–23, 1993

DON'T TAKE NO FOR AN ANSWER, BUT ALSO DON'T REACT IN ANGER. . . .

Regard every opportunity, every encounter, as an opportunity to teach someone.

Symposium at Columbia Law School,
February 10, 2012

ALL PERSONS
should care
about the
next generation.

US Supreme Court Justice
Confirmation Hearings,
July 20–23, 1993

I GOT THE IDEA THAT BEING A LAWYER IS A PRETTY GOOD THING because in addition to practicing a profession, you could do some good for your society, make things a little better for other people.

Remarks at Georgetown University Law Center,
February 4, 2015

WORK FOR THE THINGS THAT YOU CARE ABOUT.

Interview with the *New Republic*,
September 2014

People elect Members of Congress to make laws for them, **AND IF PEOPLE DON'T LIKE THOSE LAWS,** they can vote out the people who made them.

US Supreme Court Justice
Confirmation Hearings,
July 20-23, 1993

I WISH THERE WERE A WAY I COULD WAVE A MAGIC WAND AND PUT IT BACK WHEN PEOPLE WERE RESPECTFUL OF EACH OTHER AND THE CONGRESS WAS WORKING FOR THE GOOD OF THE COUNTRY AND NOT JUST ALONG PARTY LINES.

Stanford Rathbun Lecture,
February 6, 2017

TIME is on the side of CHANGE.

Interview with the *New York Times*,
July 7, 2009

Starting that
[*Notorious RBG*] Tumblr
is a good example of how
young people should react
to things they don't like.

Stanford Rathbun Lecture,
February 6, 2017

I think the Framers were intending to create a more perfect union that would become **EVER MORE PERFECT OVER TIME.**

US Supreme Court Justice
Confirmation Hearings,
July 20-23, 1993

The great thing
about our Constitution
is that, like our society,
IT CAN EVOLVE.

Stanford Rathbun Lecture,
February 6, 2017

When we no longer need people
to keep muskets in their home,
**then the Second Amendment
has no function.**

Interview with *The Takeaway*,
September 12, 2013

IF YOU'RE GOING TO CHANGE THINGS,

you have to be with the people who hold the levers.

Interview with the *New York Times*,
July 7, 2009

One of the things that I have done every other year with my law clerks . . . is to visit the local jail and Lorton Penitentiary. . . . We visited St. Elizabeth's, the facility for the criminally insane, when it was a Federal facility. . . . I do that to expose myself to those conditions, and also for my law clerks. Most of them will go on to practice in large law firms specializing in corporate business, and won't see the law as it affects most people. **THAT IS ONE OF THE THINGS I DO TO STAY IN TOUCH.**

US Supreme Court Justice
Confirmation Hearings,
July 20-23, 1993

ONE CAN HOPE
THAT WE WILL
LEARN FROM
THE HISTORY
OF THE PAST.

Interview on *NOW with Bill Moyers*,
May 3, 2002

Generally, change in our society
is incremental, I think.
REAL CHANGE, ENDURING CHANGE,
happens one step at a time.

US Supreme Court Justice
Confirmation Hearings,
July 20-23, 1993

DO SOMETHING OUTSIDE YOURSELF— something to repair tears in your community, something to make life a little better for people less fortunate than you. That's what I think a meaningful life is.

Stanford Rathbun Lecture,
February 6, 2017

ATTITUDE IS EVERYTHING

I APPRECIATE
THAT I AM NEVER
GOING TO PLEASE
**ALL OF THE PEOPLE
ALL OF THE TIME** . . .

US Supreme Court Justice
Confirmation Hearings,
July 20-23, 1993

I'm dejected, but only momentarily, when I can't get the fifth vote for something I think is very important. But then you go on to the next challenge and you give it your all. You know that these important issues are not going to go away. They are going to come back again and again. **There'll be another time, another day.**

Interview with ABC News
correspondent Lynn Sherr,
November 15, 2000

Some terrible things have happened in the United States, but one can only hope that we **learn from those bad things.**

Interview with *BBC Newsnight*,
February 23, 2017

I wondered whether I could manage Harvard Law School with an infant. My father-in-law's advice: **"You know, Ruth, if you don't want to go to law school, no one will think the less of you. You have the best reason in the world. But if that's what you want to do, if you want to be a lawyer, you will pick yourself up, you will stop feeling sorry for yourself, and you will find a way."** And that attitude is one that I have tried to maintain ever since.

Symposium at Columbia Law School,
February 10, 2012

IF I LOSE TODAY, THERE'S HOPE THAT TOMORROW WILL BE BETTER.

Symposium at Columbia Law School,
February 10, 2012

We are not experiencing the best of times, but there's hope in seeing how the public is reacting to it. . . . **THERE IS REASON TO HOPE THAT WE WILL SEE A BETTER DAY.**

Interview with *BBC Newsnight*, February 23, 2017

So often in life,
things that you regard
as an impediment
**turn out to be great
good fortune.**

A conversation with *Makers*,
June 12, 2012

We were married in Marty's home, and his mother took me into the bedroom, her bedroom, and said, **"Dear, I'd like to tell you the secret of a happy marriage. . . . It helps sometimes to be a little deaf."** And I found that advice—it stood me in very good stead not only in a wonderful marriage that lasted well over half a century, but in every workplace I've served, dealing with my faculty colleagues when I was a law teacher, and even now with my colleagues on the Supreme Court. When an unkind word is said, a thoughtless word, best to tune out.

Interview with the
American Academy of Achievement,
July 14, 2016

You can't have it all, all at once. Who—man or woman—has it all, all at once? **Over my lifespan I think I have had it all.** But in different periods of time things were rough. And if you have a caring life partner, you help the other person when that person needs it.

Yahoo! interview with Katie Couric,
July 30, 2014

It is much easier to criticize than
to come up with an alternative.
So, as a general matter,
**I would never tear down unless
I am sure I have a better
building to replace what is
being torn down.**

US Supreme Court Justice
Confirmation Hearings,
July 20–23, 1993

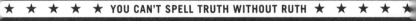
Willingness to entertain the position of the other person, readiness to rethink one's own views, are

IMPORTANT ATTITUDES ON A COLLEGIAL COURT.

US Supreme Court Justice
Confirmation Hearings,
July 20-23, 1993

A SENSE OF HUMOR HELPS ENORMOUSLY.

Stanford Rathbun Lecture,
February 6, 2017

I WILL NEVER COMPROMISE when it's a question of, say, **freedom of speech** or **press, gender equality.**

Conversation at Duke University School of Law,
July 21, 2017

I consult legislative
history with an attitude
of **hopeful skepticism.**

US Supreme Court Justice
Confirmation Hearings,
July 20–23, 1993

We must try to train ourselves and those about us to live together with one another as **good neighbors.**

Highway Herald, published by pupils of Elementary Public School 238, Brooklyn, New York, June 1946

SUPREME
LIFE LESSONS

AS WE LIVE, WE CAN LEARN. IT'S IMPORTANT TO LISTEN.

Interview with Irin Carmon
on *The Rachel Maddow Show*,
February 16, 2015

WHEREVER YOU ARE, WHATEVER YOUR AUDIENCE IS, you want to play to that audience and not turn it against you.

Interview prior to the Inaugural
Justice Ruth Bader Ginsburg Distinguished
Lecture on Women and the Law,
November 15, 2000

Anger is a useless emotion—
it doesn't advance your cause.

Stanford Rathbun Lecture,
February 6, 2017

NEVER WRITE A SENTENCE that has to be read again to be understood.

Symposium at Columbia Law School,
February 10, 2012

I hope what I write has staying power.

Symposium at Columbia Law School,
February 10, 2012

I got very good advice when I became a judge of the D.C. circuit. My senior colleague said, **"RUTH, I'M GONNA TELL YOU SOMETHING ABOUT THE BUSINESS OF JUDGING. YOU WORK VERY HARD ON EACH CASE. BUT WHEN IT'S OVER, DON'T LOOK BACK. DON'T WORRY ABOUT THINGS THAT ARE OVER AND DONE. IT'S NOT PRODUCTIVE TO DO THAT."**

Interview with Irin Carmon
on *The Rachel Maddow Show*,
February 16, 2015

Before the start of each day in Court, and before each conference discussion, . . . **we shake hands, each Justice with every other.**

Remarks presented to the
Association of Business Trial Lawyers,
February 8, 2013

WASTE NO TIME
on anger,
regret,
or resentment,
JUST GET THE
JOB DONE.

Remarks delivered at the National Museum
of Women and the Arts in Washington, D.C.,
April 15, 2015

I've gotten much more
satisfaction for the things
that I've done for which
I was not paid.

Interview with Irin Carmon
on *The Rachel Maddow Show*,
February 16, 2015

COURTING
JUSTICE

If you took a poll today of
the three branches of government,
which one do the people think
is doing the best job?

We're way out in front of Congress.

Remarks at Georgetown Law School,
September 20, 2017

What a judge should
take account of is not
the weather of the day,
**BUT THE CLIMATE
OF AN ERA.**

US Supreme Court Justice
Confirmation Hearings,
July 20-23, 1993

CONSTANT REALIZATION OF A MORE PERFECT UNION, the Constitution's aspiration, requires the widest, broadest, deepest participation on matters of government and government policy.

US Supreme Court Justice
Confirmation Hearings,
July 20–23, 1993

IT MUST START WITH THE PEOPLE. LEGISLATURES ARE NOT GOING TO MOVE WITHOUT THAT KIND OF PROPULSION.

Interview with the *New Republic*,
September 2014

Our system of justice is surely richer for the **diversity of background and experience** of its judges.

Remarks presented to the American Sociological Association Annual Meeting, August 11, 2006

If there is any message
I would like the public to
understand about courts,
it is that **courts don't make
controversies; courts don't
choose what they do.**

US Supreme Court Justice
Confirmation Hearings,
July 20-23, 1993

JUSTICES CONTINUE TO THINK AND CAN CHANGE....

I am ever hopeful that if the court has a blind spot today, its eyes will be open tomorrow.

Yahoo! interview with Katie Couric,
July 30, 2014

Supreme Court Justices...

continuously confront matters
on which the Framers left things
unsaid, unsettled, or uncertain.

US Supreme Court Justice
Confirmation Hearings,
July 20-23, 1993

When you're writing for a collegial court, you're never writing just for yourself. **You can't write the opinion as you would if you were queen.**

Symposium at Columbia Law School,
February 10, 2012

Judges must be mindful of their place in our constitutional order; they must always remember that we live in a democracy that can be destroyed if judges take it upon themselves to rule as Platonic guardians.

US Supreme Court Justice
Confirmation Hearings,
July 20-23, 1993

The plaintiffs I represented were extraordinary people in the sense that **THEY HAD FAITH IN OUR SYSTEM OF JUSTICE** and **HAD THE BRAVERY TO TEST THAT FAITH.**

Gruber Distinguished Lecture in Women's Rights,
hosted by Yale Law School,
October 19, 2012

The controversies that come to the Supreme Court, as the last judicial resort, touch and concern the health and well-being of our nation and its people. They affect the preservation of liberty to ourselves and our posterity. **Serving on this Court is the highest honor, the most awesome trust, that can be placed in a judge.**

US Supreme Court Justice
Confirmation Hearings,
July 20-23, 1993

We serve no client, our commission is to do what's right—what the law requires and what is just.

Remarks presented to the Wake Forest University School of Law Summer Program in Venice, Italy, July 2016

IT'S THE BEST AND THE HARDEST JOB I'VE EVER HAD.

Gruber Distinguished Lecture in Women's Rights,
hosted by Yale Law School,
October 19, 2012

I don't cry anymore, but I still . . .
every time I'm part of that
process [a death penalty case],
I am unsettled, unsettled by it.

Interview on *NOW with Bill Moyers*,
May 3, 2002

I am sometimes asked:
"Don't you miss advocacy?"
When the Court is divided, my
role resembles an advocate's.

Gruber Distinguished Lecture in Women's Rights,
hosted by Yale Law School,
October 19, 2012

COURTS WILL WORK OUT A REMEDY THEMSELVES ONLY AS THE VERY LAST RESORT, after trying in every way possible to have the people's elected representatives do the job that they should do.

US Supreme Court Justice
Confirmation Hearings,
July 20–23, 1993

**We care about this institution
more than our individual egos**
and we are all devoted to keeping the
Supreme Court in the place that it is, as
a co-equal third branch of government
and I think a model for the world in the
collegiality and independence of judges.

Interview with C-SPAN,
July 1, 2009

I have only one passion and it is **to be a good judge,** to judge fairly.

US Supreme Court Justice
Confirmation Hearings,
July 20-23, 1993

QUEEN

OF THE

DISSENT

Some of my favorite opinions are dissenting opinions. I will not live to see what becomes of them, but I . . . I remain hopeful.

Interview on *NOW with Bill Moyers*,
May 3, 2002

My dissenting opinions, like my briefs, are intended to persuade. **AND SOMETIMES ONE MUST BE FORCEFUL ABOUT SAYING HOW WRONG THE COURT'S DECISION IS.**

Interview with the *New Republic*,
September 2014

I WILL NEVER, as long as I am able to sit on any court, rule the way the home crowd wants out of concern about how it will play in the press if I rule the other way.

US Supreme Court Justice
Confirmation Hearings,
July 20-23, 1993

Dissents speak to a future age. It's not simply to say my colleagues are wrong and I would do it this way, but the greatest dissents do become court opinions.

Interview on *NOW with Bill Moyers*,
May 3, 2002

Throwing out preclearance when it has worked and is continuing to work to stop discriminatory changes is **LIKE THROWING AWAY YOUR UMBRELLA IN A RAINSTORM BECAUSE YOU ARE NOT GETTING WET.**

Shelby County v. Holder Dissent,
June 25, 2013

Just as buildings in California have a greater need to be earthquake-proofed, places where there is greater racial polarization in voting **have a greater need for prophylactic measures to prevent purposeful race discrimination.**

Shelby County v. Holder Dissent,
June 25, 2013

In our view, the Court does not comprehend, or is indifferent to, **the insidious way in which women can be victims of pay discrimination.**

Ledbetter v. Goodyear Tire & Rubber Co. Bench Announcement, May 29, 2007

The greatest threat to public confidence in elections in this case is the prospect of enforcing a purposefully discriminatory law, **one that likely imposes an unconstitutional poll tax** and **risks denying the right to vote to hundreds of thousands of eligible voters.**

Veasy v. Perry Dissent,
October 18, 2014

Religious organizations exist to foster the interests of persons subscribing to the same religious faith. Not so of for-profit corporations. Workers who sustain the operations of those corporations commonly are not drawn from one religious community. **INDEED, BY LAW, NO RELIGION-BASED CRITERION CAN RESTRICT THE WORK FORCE OF FOR-PROFIT CORPORATIONS.**

Burwell v. Hobby Lobby Dissent,
June 30, 2014

And where is the stopping point...?

Suppose it offends an employer's religious belief to pay the minimum wage, or to accord women equal pay for substantially similar work?

Burwell v. Hobby Lobby Bench Announcement,
June 30, 2014

THE COURT, I FEAR, HAS VENTURED INTO A MINEFIELD.

Burwell v. Hobby Lobby Dissent,
June 30, 2014

The stain of generations of racial oppression is still visible in our society . . . **and the determination to hasten its removal remains vital.**

Gratz v. Bollinger Dissent,
June 23, 2003

As anyone with employment experience can easily grasp, in-charge employees authorized to assign and control subordinate employees' daily work are aided in accomplishing their harassment by the superintending position in which their employer places them, **AND FOR THAT REASON, THE EMPLOYER IS PROPERLY HELD RESPONSIBLE FOR THE MISCONDUCT.**

Vance v. Ball State University Bench Announcement, June 24, 2013

YOU'RE SAYING... THERE ARE TWO KINDS OF MARRIAGE: THE FULL MARRIAGE AND THEN THIS SORT OF SKIM-MILK MARRIAGE.

Oral arguments in *United States v. Windsor*,
March 27, 2013

The Court's majority would compare health insurance to broccoli. If the government can compel people to buy insurance, then there is no commodity the government can't force people to purchase, so the argument goes. **But health care is not like vegetables. . . . All of us will need health care, some sooner, some later.**

National Federation of Independent Business v. Sebelius Bench Announcement, June 28, 2012

Yes, the insurance purchase mandate is novel, but novelty is no reason to reject it. As our economy grows and changes, **Congress must be competent to devise legislation meeting current-day social and economic realities.**

National Federation of Independent Business v. Sebelius Bench Announcement, June 28, 2012

Such an untested prophecy **should not decide the Presidency of the United States.**

Bush v. Gore dissent,
December 12, 2000

THE RUTH
BOOSTER CLUB

My mother told me two things constantly. **One was to be a lady, and the other was to be independent.** . . . . For most girls growing up in the '40s, the most important degree was not your B.A., but your M.R.S.

via ACLU

Neither of my parents had the means
to attend college, but both taught me to
**LOVE LEARNING, TO CARE ABOUT
PEOPLE, AND TO WORK HARD** for
whatever I wanted or believed in.

US Supreme Court Justice
Confirmation Hearings,
July 20-23, 1993

In her high school yearbook on her graduation in 1973, the listing for Jane Ginsburg under **"ambition"** was **"to see her mother appointed to the Supreme Court."** The next line read, **"IF NECESSARY, JANE WILL APPOINT HER."**

US Supreme Court Justice
Nomination Acceptance Address,
June 14, 1993

I surely would not be in this room today—without the determined efforts of men and women who kept dreams of equal citizenship alive in days when few would listen. People like **SUSAN B. ANTHONY, ELIZABETH CADY STANTON,** and **HARRIET TUBMAN** come to mind. I stand on the shoulders of those brave people.

US Supreme Court Justice
Confirmation Hearings,
July 20-23, 1993

I vividly remember the day I opened
New York magazine and found the
first issue of ***Ms.* magazine** inside.

Remarks presented to the New York City
Bar Association, introducing Gloria Steinem,
February 2, 2015

IT'S HARD TO DO ANYTHING ALONE. BUT GET TOGETHER WITH LIKE-MINDED PEOPLE, **JOIN ORGANIZATIONS.**

Stanford Rathbun Lecture,
February 6, 2017

I have had the great fortune to share life with a partner truly extraordinary for his generation, a man who believed . . .

that a woman's work— at home or on the job— is as important as a man's.

US Supreme Court Justice
Confirmation Hearings,
July 20-23, 1993

[Marty] was the only boy I had met up until then who **CARED THAT I HAD A BRAIN.**

Equal Justice Works event,
October 27, 2017

I think that most girls who grew up when I did were very fond of the Nancy Drew series. Not because they were well written, they weren't, but because this was a girl who was **AN ADVENTURER, WHO COULD THINK FOR HERSELF, WHO WAS THE DOMINANT PERSON IN HER RELATIONSHIP** with her young boyfriend. So the Nancy Drew series made girls feel good, that they could be achievers and they didn't have to take a back seat or be wallflowers.

Interview with American
Academy of Achievement,
July 14, 2016

In those days, I had one fictional hero—**Nancy Drew**—and one real one, that was **Amelia Earhart.**

Equal Justice Works event,
October 27, 2017

THE BEST ADVICE I GOT WAS FROM JUSTICE O'CONNOR, who had taken her seat on the bench at an oral argument just nine days after her breast cancer surgery. "Ruth," she counseled, "you're going to get reams of mail from well-wishers. Don't even try to respond. Just concentrate on the Court's work." And she added, "Schedule chemotherapy for Fridays. Use the weekend to get over it, and be back in Court on Monday."

Gruber Distinguished Lecture in Women's Rights,
hosted by Yale Law School,
October 19, 2012

I can say one thing about Justice Scalia: He is one of the few people in the world who can make me laugh, and I appreciate him for that.

US Supreme Court Justice
Confirmation Hearings,
July 20–23, 1993

My children decided at an early age that mother's sense of humor needed improvement. They tried to supply that improvement, and kept a book to record their successes.

THE BOOK WAS CALLED "MOMMY LAUGHED."

US Supreme Court Justice
Confirmation Hearings,
July 20-23, 1993

THE
NOTORIOUS
RBG

IF I HAD ANY TALENT THAT GOD COULD GIVE ME, I WOULD BE A GREAT DIVA.

Remarks at Georgetown University Law Center,
February 4, 2015

We do ten [pushups] at a time.
And then I breathe for a bit and
do the second set.

Interview on *The Rachel Maddow Show*,
February 16, 2015

John Paul Stevens didn't step down [from the Supreme Court] until he was 90.

Interview with the *New York Times*,
February 20, 2015

There is only one prediction that is entirely safe about the upcoming term, and that is **IT WILL BE MOMENTOUS.**

Remarks at Georgetown Law School,
September 20, 2017

At my advanced age—I'm now an octogenarian—**I'm constantly amazed by the number of people who want to take my picture.**

Interview with the *New Republic*,
September 2014

As for the mugs and
the T-shirts, that is fine,
but the tattoo…
that is a bit much.

Lecture at the European University Institute in Italy,
February 2016

Who do you think Obama could
have nominated **AND GOT CONFIRMED**
that you'd rather see on a court?

Interview with the *New York Times*,
February 20, 2015

I AM THOUGHT OF AS A JUDGE, WHO HAPPENS TO BE A WOMAN.

US Supreme Court Justice
Confirmation Hearings,
July 20-23, 1993

You can tell them **I'll be back** doing push-ups next week.

Remarks to creators of the
Notorious RBG Tumblr after stent surgery,
December 10, 2014

I probably read
more fiction **because
I deal every day with
so much nonfiction.**

US Supreme Court Justice
Confirmation Hearings,
July 20-23, 1993

HOW DID I DECIDE TO BECOME A FLAMING FEMINIST LITIGATOR?

Remarks at Georgetown University Law School,
September 20, 2017

I tried out student teaching

. . . and didn't love it. Plus I was supposed
to teach about the Spanish-American War.
I got the syllabus, and it said everything the
United States did was right and everything
the other side did was wrong. And I knew
that history is not that way.

Equal Justice Works event,
October 27, 2017

Someday there will be great people, great elected representatives who will say, **"Enough of this nonsense. Let's be the kind of legislature the United States should have."** I hope that day will come while I'm still alive.

Stanford Rathbun Lecture,
February 6, 2017

I would like to be thought of as someone who cares about people AND DOES THE BEST SHE CAN with the talent she has to make a contribution to a better world.

US Supreme Court Justice
Confirmation Hearings,
July 20-23, 1993

All I can say is that I AM STILL HERE and likely to remain for a while.

Yahoo! interview with Katie Couric,
July 30, 2014

THERE IS STILL WORK TO BE DONE.

Roosevelt University's 2017
American Dream Reconsidered conference,
September 11, 2017

As long as I can do the job full steam, I WILL DO IT.

Equal Justice Works event,
October 27, 2017